JOURNEY

OF

LIFE

By
Ilana R. Lunn

Expanded Edition

ISBN: 978-0-9908615-1-5

Dedication

Greg Lunn
Beloved husband

Special thanks to Barr Batzer for the cover design.

TABLE OF CONTENTS

LIFE DEFINED

Its beauty,

Its splendor,

Its magnificence,

All add to its fancy.

Its poverty,

Its greed,

Its war,

All add to its gloom.

Its glory,

Its people,

Its love,

All add to its victory.

Its fancy,

Its gloom,

Its victory,

All add to its life.

LIFE

Life,
What is life?

Life,
Life is full of tragedies.

Life,
Life is full of miseries.

Life,
Why was I born in this world?

Life,
This world is full of greediness.

Life,
Where is all the happiness?

Life,
Why are people born every day?

Life,
Why do people die every day?

Life,
Why did you kill my family?

Life,
Take me, too!

THE ABERDABBER TREE

On the highest low mountain

Deeper than the eye can see

Where you can see

Darker than dark

Where you can see

The sun never shines

But lighted by rock

Through the paths of death

Past the cloud stairs

Over the swamps

Under the moors

Below the vast fields

Beyond the depths of the forest

Betwixt the willows and the reeds

You shall find the Aberdabber Tree.

PERFECTION

Oh, woesome me!
My life is a ruin.
Vision of perfection
Hearing acute
None so good as
Smell and taste
Touch sensitive.
Beauty!
As never seen before.
Fame! Fortune!
All was mine, but
Blotted was my mind.
Lonesome life
Surrounding fire
They warned me
But I did not here
Nor did I see.
It stank sour
But I did not smell
Nor did I taste.
It was scratch rough
But I did not touch
Nor did I care.
Oh, damn my mind!
My life is a ruin.

HEARTACHE

Oh, wounded is my heart!
Blind was I
To his grueling ways.

Oh, the sorrow of it all.
How could I have permit him?
My soul is devastated.

I knew it was wrong
Listen I to myself? -No
How foolish I had been!

My life is changed.
Ruined I am
Death is the sole answer.

That scoundrel!
Why? -It is not fair
He killed my soul.

Wretched and heartbroken am I!
Forgive me, my Lord
For I was deceived.

FLYING HIGH

I'm going to fly to the woods,
Flitter, flatter,
Flitter, flatter.
I'll spread my arms,
Flap, flap.

Slowly I'll rise from the ground,
Swoop into air,
Under and above
Tree branches.

The leaves brush against my wings;
My wings of freedom
As I go soaring to the sky,
Gliding
Flitter, flatter.

Flap, flap
Through the clouds
Gentle, calm,
Faster,
Flitter, flap,
Fierce, wild.

Beyond the clouds,
Closer to the outer region;
Faster, fiercer,
Flitter, flap.

Hitting the atmosphere,
Stars ahead,
The universe for my desire!

Breaking out-
Faster, swifter,
Flitter, flatter,
Flap, flap,
Fiercer, wilder-
Out there at last
I'll explode;
Blood splattering,
Millions of pieces
Floating,
Gliding
Through the universe.
Freedom at last!

Yes, I will.
I'm going to fly to the woods,
Flitter, flatter,
Flitter, flatter.

NATURE

Whispering willows sway silently

   in the breeze

   blowing the leaves.

White water flows freely

   with leaping frogs

   over the logs.

Frolicking fish swim sweetly

   under lily pads

   hiding from lads.

Elegant existence lives listfully

   where Nature knows

   Only It grows.

HEAVENS ABOVE

Sun shines bright

   wherever it might;

Moon may light

   on lovers' delight;

Stars sing night

   all seem right;

But the sky

   wants to cry.

TICK TICK TOCK

Time and time again
Eternity hails
Stopping short;

So much to learn
No time to teach...

Birds chirp the mornings away
While owls whoo the nights;

So much in life
No time to waste
Hands of infinity
Keep us ticking
On our rocks...

Some clocks are slow
Some clocks are fast
Some clocks never move
Some clocks never stop;

Waiting
Relentlessly longing
Yet fearfully dreading...

All will eventually meet their tock.

SERENITY

Alone

The still dock across the water

Fog drifting through the light

Empty cliffs beneath the dark sky

Drip dropping in a nearby fountain

The only sound;

Rocking chairs with no life

Occasional people passing by

Cold and dry in the moist air

Bright warmth within not so far;

A tear falls at the sound of others laughing

A tear falls for memories

A tear falls in loneliness.

ELECTRIC SOUL

The wind thrashes the pouring rain
A sea upon the street of sailing cars
People swimming for shelter;

Lightning flashes
Thunder purrs
Continuing...
BANG!
FLASH!
Thunder purrs....

I reach out my hand
Thunderous vibrations
BANG!
FLASH!
Electricity surges through body and mind
While thunder and soul become one...!

Vibrating together
Lightning flashes
BANG!
FLASH!
Live thunder, live!

Wind winding down...
Flashes diminish
Thunder purrs
Softly...
Away away to catch the hearts of other souls....

But my soul yet lives
Still thundering...

Thundering feline
Body flashing!
Mind soaring!

The storm has left its mark
As it will with many....

DISILLUSIONED

Death glooms over
What is there in life?
Mistreatment
Insensitivity

Foolhardy trusting those
Insensitive traitors who call themselves
Friends

Friend
Abstract concept
Does not truly exist
True friends
Will never exist.

To believe one has a
True friendship
Lives in a fantasy.

SILENT VOICE

I am not stupid
I am as smart as you
Intelligent, in fact.

Though I speak not
I can think
The same answers come to me
But may be at a slower rate.

I am just as good as you
Don't put me down for not having a voice
My voice is silent
It is afraid to be heard
Afraid of being wrong
Or being put down.

Perhaps you have already
Spoken my thoughts
Why should I repeat
That already heard?

Perhaps I have no new ideas
Perhaps I do
And if I do -why should I tell them to you?
They may inspire you, or
You may put them down.

But they are my ideas
They are the product of me-
My intelligence
My character
My sense of the world

Put simply-
Me.

If you put me down because
I am different
Then do I not have the
Privilege to do the same
To you for the
Same reason?

We are only human-
All human
Because we are different does
Not make one better than the other.

Intelligence has many meanings
Your intelligence may reside in
One area, while mine is in
Yet another.

Perhaps we are different in
Many ways: looks, thoughts,
Personalities, morals, beliefs
Raised in different cultures?
Different societies?
Different people?

But do human differences give you
The right -the privilege-
To put me down?

Accept me as I am
I am only different
I am me.

BEFORE BREAKFAST

Early morn
The sun has risen.
A bird fly's by
Above me
Under the blue sky
With powder white clouds.
A man
Stands upon the deck
With his fishing pole
In the lake.
Sound of birds all
Around the house
And mountain.
Cool breeze rippling the
Clear lake beyond me.
I wish for a
Nickel
To buy some pellets
To feed the fish
Below me
And my perch above
The calm still water.

I take in the
Fresh air into
Tired lungs
Relaxing the nerves that
Refused to sleep and
Woke me
Up thus so early.
But perhaps
It is not bad

I awoke before the
Alarm clock.
Now I get the
Chance to see Nature
In its
Early morning splendor,
A beautiful sight to
See.
Perfect way to calm
My angered nerves and
Greet the
New day with clear
Mind and calm thoughts.

THE GAZEBO

Sitting in a gazebo:
Birds chirping in the distance,
My brother flipping pages of his book,
The only sounds I hear.
I lean against a post.
Eyes on the calm water
With light rippling,
A bird flutters by.
Sudden "olayhoos" of my comrade
Echo over the lake and
Over the mountains
Reaching for the sky.

I gaze at the varying lake:
Across the way
Dark green reflections of the trees;
A stream of sparkling bright stars,
Running from the many ripples
To the light ripples
Ending below the rock of the
Gazebo we inhabit

INNER PEACE

Sitting here
In the cool breeze
By some rocks
Next to the calm lake,
I feel connected,
Connected to all.
From the spider
Hanging above nearby
To homo-sapiens
To the clouds
In the sky,
All part of
The same world.
Nature nourishes
From the one-celled
To the many-celled.
Animals, plants
And minerals
Interacting in
Living and depending on
Where all are equal
And whole in
Nature

NATURE'S ROCKING CHAIR

Escape-
Gray clouds drifting over a serene mountain,
Tree branches wavering in the breeze,
Light drizzle dropping in the calm lake.
Dock all empty and wet
With a pot of pink flowers
Next to a bench.
Wherever I look
There is green,
Full and majestic
Green trees,
Topped by a tower high up
Reaching for the clouds.

Alone
I sit here
Rocking
In my own thoughts
In my own world
In Nature.

Elating
Enlightening
My wings open once again.
Lost in thought
I find myself floating,
Floating over the calm rippling lake
Past the dock,
Higher,
My wings brush against the trees.
I spot a bird nearby,
We exchange glances.

Floating higher,
Higher than the mountain
So near the clouds.

My spirit is elated
Lost in my own world.
No one to disrupt
My thoughts,
My feelings,
I am alone.

Mother Nature embraces me.
She soothes my pain
With her wondrous beauty
And power.
I become a whole being in
Nature's lap.

Nature fills my spirit with Her spirit
Lost in the world of Nature
Enlightened once more with
Peace of mind.

TRAPPED

I sit here
My legs crossed
Indian-style
On the corner
Of the ledge
By the lake.
I see the woods,
Stone and trees,
The tower above.
I think of the
Reservoir with the
Frogs and lily-pads.
I remember walking
Within those woods
On that mountain.
But this year
I cannot.
My illness
Keeps me still,
Cannot walk far
Due to quick fatigue.
I ache in
Yearning to walk
Amongst Nature,
But I cannot.
So I sit here
On the ledge
In a corner.
Dreaming,
Taking in the view,
Observing stars appearing
In the night sky,

I close my eyes.
Walking and climbing
In the woods,
Higher and higher,
I reach the top.
Climb the stairs
Within the tower,
I feel power
Up here,
Beautiful and endless sights.
Enlightened spirit,
I open my eyes.
Next year
You can do it.
Next year
You'll have
Energy once more.

LITTLE TREE IN THE WOODS

My name
Who I am
A little tree
Living in a jungle
Full of trees
Larger and smaller
Than I

But

We are all one
One tree
One name
Doing one thing

Trying to survive

Struggling through
Woods
Tangled in
One enormous jungle

With little hope of escape
Fighting for life
Or deserting the forests
Running away for fear
From all the trees

To be your own tree
A single tree
At peace
No others to trouble you

But

There is loneliness
Result of aloneness
Needing others

That single little tree
Returns ready for the fight
With renewed strength
Joins other little trees
Helping each other survive

In the thick woods

Of the world

A DARK CAFÉ

Sitting here
Coca cola
The closest I feel
My best friend
Here
In this coffee shop
Amongst friends
Met tonight

Sometimes alone

Sometimes in company

Confusion
Shyness

Fear

Friend who brought me
He left
Went to the game room

I came here
With him

I'm with
His friends

My new friends
Welcoming
Me
With open arms

His last girlfriend is
Here
She and two
Others
Are with him

I want to cry
I want to call
My Daddy
And cry

Relieve the
Tension
Fear

I need a
Hug

Please

Someone

Help me

BLANK LOOKS

A space opens
In the crowd
I move
Bump into someone
Doing the same
Behind me

I turn reflexively
He turns as well

We look at each other
No acknowledgement
No blame
No anger
Nothing

Emotionless stares
For five seconds

We turn back to our own business

FEELINGS 1

This feeling
No stranger
To me

Wonderful feeling
Always makes
Me feel
Happy
Like a

Whole being

It scares me
Though

Whenever I
Experience this
Feeling
It hurts evermore

In the end

MEMORIES NEVER DIE

An old lady sits in the corner
Of a sitting room in the nursing home
Her face is shrunken and wrinkled
Around weary gray eyes
And tight sucked-in mouth
Grayish-white hair thinning
Above her forehead and ears
Her expression tells of
Loneliness and a lost past

Her granddaughter has come to visit
Placing her own young baby
Into her grandmother's arms
The old lady looks down
Into the infant's bright blue eyes
She observes the full cheeks
And fresh pink skin drawn in
By a toothless mouth

The baby's hand reaches up
Her tiny fingers feeling the wrinkles
On her great-grandmother's face
The lady smiles
It is a smile full of love and
Memories

Young and old eyes meet
Generations join as one
As old memories become a part of
New memories soon to be formed
The young infant returns the same youthful smile
To her great-grandmother's gleaming eyes
Gleaming with life

The old lady strokes the baby's face
Sharing her life with her youngest born descendent

SECRET DREAMS I

The earth called to me today

Come hither
I want to tell you a secret

It whispered so softly

See the trees towering high in the sky
Above the green grass you walk upon

Notice the fields of flowers
In rainbows of colors

Observe the diverse birds
Among the clouds and the ground

Catch sight of the large and small animals
Skittering and sneaking around

Look in at yourself

The earth was silent then

I paused
I looked within myself

It occurred to me what
The secret was

I spoke to the earth

I am as a tall tree

Walking on the short grass below me

I am but one flower
In a field of flowers

I am a bird who flies high in the sky
With my feet yet on the ground

I am an animal preying on smaller animals than I
While larger animals are doing the same to me

The earth remained silent

I am human
An interactive part of Nature

The earth spoke

All the plants
All the birds

All the fish
And all the animals

Are my children

I embrace them all
With equal care

Can you tell me the secret?

I remained silent

No part of Nature

Is more important than another

They need each other
To live and thrive

Every plant and animal
Plays a role in Nature

Do you understand the secret now
My child?

Yes, Mother Earth, I understand

The earth embraced me in her mighty arms

LITTLE CHILD

Little child
So lost and alone
Run along home
There are people who love you
Wondering where you have gone off

Little child
So lost and alone
Let those who care
Help you find yourself
Discover who you really are

Little child
So lost and alone
Come share your feelings
You are not alone in this cold and harsh world
With those who care

Little child
So lost and alone
Sit by my side
Let your tears flow
For I am with you always

YOU ARE WITHIN ME

Wherever I look
There you are
Wherever I turn
I see your eyes

I hear your soothing voice
Whenever I am troubled
Chiming through my heart
You're there for me

In a field of sweet flowers
Or congested from a cold
I know your scent
Filling me with love

Your gentle hugs and caresses
I feel the whole day through
No matter how many miles far apart
Your touch is a thought away

The taste of your lips
Brushing against mine
I inhale your sweet breath
Absorbing your comforting words

I close my eyes
Spinning in silence
Lost in an empty world
Full of clouds

A hand reaches out
I feel it deep inside me
When I'm all alone
Scared of opening my eyes

Shining bright within the darkness
Touching my fears gently

Embracing me with love
Tenderness pouring from your touch

Hand in hand
You open my eyes slowly
I see your smiling face
Causing me to smile

Your loving eyes seep through mine
Calming my fears
I cry on your shoulder
My heart and soul

WINGED SPIRIT

Don't hide away
Tucked in a dark corner
Keeping to yourself
Holding back your dreams

Set your spirit free
Spread your wings
Don't hide your colors
In the dreary blackness

Embrace the world
Show them who you are
Be proud of yourself
Blind them with your light

You are who you are
Do not be ashamed
Change is not necessary
Just be yourself

Let them see
You are proud
Proud of who you are
What you are

Get those wings flying
Fill the air with your breeze
Blowing them away
With your spirit

So take my hand
I'll help you

Find yourself
Beyond the dark shadows

In the light of day
You'll shine
Brighter than the sun
As you spread your wings

ETERNITY

Love is not easy for everyone to express
I know this from personal experience
Feelings are very strong and true
But expressing them to a loved one
Is not an easy thing

Love comes from the heart
But it is more than a feeling
More than a word from the heart
It requires nurturing
An expression of how much we care

Cherish every moment
Find ways to express your love
For all the cherished ones
Residing in your heart
Whether they know it or not

Spend time with a loved one
Be there for his downs in life
As well as his ups
Share yourself with him
And he will share with you

Life does not last an eternity
But love can last for many eternities
Cherish every moment with a loved one
No matter who they are
No matter the distance between you

Love brings spirits together
It keeps us going throughout life's trials
There is always room for love
Deep in the heart and soul
So don't keep your heart locked

For some it is easy

For others it is difficult
But there are three simple words
That express it all for someone you care for
"I love you"

TEARS SHALL FLOW

Pain...it's always there
Whether we know it or not
Sometimes suppressed
Sometimes visible
But it is there

It must not be kept inside
Express your feelings
Let them out
Tears shall flow down
Don't hold back your tears

Crying is good for the soul
Release your pain
Share it with me
And I will share my pain with you
Together we can help each other

I can hear the pain in your voice
You try to hide it from me
But you cannot
I know you too well
Open your heart to me

Crying is not a bad thing
It'll help you feel better
Just burst out with those built up tears
I am here for you
No matter what the pain is

Come sit beside me
I shall embrace you in my arms

As you let your pain flow from your eyes
When you are finished crying
I will see your sweet smile once more

A WHOLE NEW WORLD

We are born with an endless imagination
Over time, the doors to this imagination are shut
And eventually locked
Each individual holds the key to unlock her door

Some people have lost their keys for life
Others can find them if they look
Then the ones like me hold the key in the palm of their hand
Take the key and unlock a whole new world

Do not be frightened of what's behind the doors
It is your own world
You control it however you like
No one can steal your key

Choose any door you like
A different adventure exists behind each one
And ever more doors behind each door
To bring you in deeper and deeper

There is no limit to the doors of imagination
Just take the key in your hand and unlock that first door
And you're on your way
To a whole new world

PAINTING

Sitting on the edge of a porch fence
Watching the sun set in the horizon
My soul is lifted from my body
I close my eyes smiling
Spiritualness fills me
Swimming in a dark pool of colors
Changing to outer space
The stars spin around in a tunnel
I am carried by some force
Through the spinning tunnel of stars
There is a light at the end
Getting brighter and brighter as I approach
At the end I am overwhelmed with a painting
Yellow surrounds me with spots
Red, orange, blue and green
I see many people in the painting
It seems like a mural of life
Millions of little people depicted in this yellow painting
All around me wherever I look I see this painting

Until I am suddenly awakened
I sit on the porch fence dreaming about the vision
Wishing to return to the painting

YOU ARE HIS MOTHER

We don't always get along
There has always been a strain between us
A person we love so much
You gave him life
Raised him through childhood
Now he turns to me
I cherish him like you do
No, I don't love him the same way
For I am not his mother
You are his mother
And I would never try to take your place
Please don't resent me or accuse me
For taking him away
You are his mother and always will be
I am his wife to be
He loves you very much
And always will
Though we are a great distance from you
You are always in our hearts
Every day and every night
He is not the greatest writer
And he is not fond of talking on the phone
But you are there in his heart always
Over time, I've come to love you
As my second mother
I hope you've come to accept me as well
As the mother of my love
Your thoughts and acceptance of me are very important
You are his mother
And I am his wife to be

YOU ARE DYING

Death
Powerful and fearful
How can I face it?
You are dying
I am helpless
Hardly 2 years ago
When we first met
You are my second mother
I don't know how
To deal with your death
You are dying
I feel it in my heart
And it scares me
Tears well up in my eyes
Just thinking of it
You are dying
How much pain are you in?
So weak and fragile
All your children have left home
Life is draining from you
Do you even care to live?
Your children love you
Your grandchildren love you
I love you

VISIONS

What's happening?
Is it simply a dream
Or is it real?
I am so frightened
To know the truth
Please tell me
If what's in my mind
Is reality or fantasy?

TRAPPED MEMORIES

No escape

Trapped
Forced

Then blamed

No one to turn to

All alone

Memories all so vivid
Tugging at your heart
Drawing tears to your eyes
For so many years

Hatred
Anger

Will you ever be able to forgive him?

NEVER ALONE

FOR BONNIE

In times of suffering
A smile is hard to hold
We wonder whether we're coming or going
Though surrounded by friends
Loneliness haunts us
Tears cover our cheeks
Fear inhabits our minds

But take heart
For we are never alone
God knows each of us more than anyone else
He knows our hearts and minds
Our feelings and thoughts are not hidden
When we are suffering He embraces us
Wiping our tears one at a time

Though our lives may seem to be ripping at the seams
The Creator has needle and thread
Holding us together with His everlasting love
Through all our tribulations
So lift up your eyes to heaven
Express all you are feeling and
Let Him comfort you in your suffering

MISERY

How can I go on?
How can I live?
I'm so alone
My home is empty
There is no comfort

Where do I go?
What do I do?
My heart is so broken
Nothing can help
I'm lost

Darkness grips my soul
Let me rot away
In a dark corner
Curled up
Crying

I feel like I can't go on
Only one person can comfort me
I'm so alone without him
Misery resides in me
My comforter isn't home

How can I go on?

WINGS OF GOLD

IN MEMORY OF BONNIE

Fly bird fly
Set your blue eyes on heaven
Let your wings of gold carry you high
You've led such a life
Now it's time to rest

You will be missed
Your smile could brighten any day
Laughs we used to share
Will always be remembered
By fellow birds and others

Oh fly bird fly
Your long suffering has come to an end
Eternal peace has come at last
Your bright eyes and brilliant smile
Will always be remembered

SILLY SECRETS

Just a little bunny hop
Or a quick Macarena
A talking teddy bear
Or a silly face and voice

You know the secret
For you alone can make me laugh
When the world around me
Makes me cry

It's your smile
And your laugh
It's your child within
And your silly antics

It's all wrapped in love
Between you and me

OUT OF CONTROL

Delusions poured in my skull
Chaos is within my soul
Am I crazy?
The world-my world is
Spinning in circles
Through dizzying depths
Away, I want to run away
This life on earth is hectic
Won't someone save me,
Calm my pounding deluded mind?
I can't stop
Spinning down in spirals
To the utter depths of the pit
Grab me, lift me up
Before I fall completely
Wacked out and lost
Won't someone help me?

SPIRALING THOUGHTS

Bind me, Save me
I am lost, out of control
Helpless in heart
Mind full of delusions
The world is a blur
My vision is unclear
I cannot think straight
Spiraling in circles
My mind is dizzy
Where am I ?
Where am I going ?
Home, I want to go home
End my mental torture
It wreaks havoc in my life
My very inner being
My behavior is crazy
Make it stop, I want to get off
Into His hands and
Rest in peace eternally

PHOTOS OF A LIFETIME

Photos of a lifetime ago
Black and white images
Forever etched in time
Look at the love, the joy
The serenity
What color is your life?
Is it all over the place,
Or in a serene surrounding?
There's life in those photos
Images of a time gone by
I wish to be there again
My heart was there that day
Happy, joyful, full of love
I relive that day
Trying to grasp myself of then
But it is just out of reach
I touch it, it moves farther away
Will I ever catch up with it,
Will I ever feel that way again?
Only time will tell of the
Emotions bogging me down
Here and forevermore

LOSS

Suffering long
Through the night
I cry out
In agony
Blind stabbing pain
Jarring my nerves
Barely moving
Lifting my eyes
Wailing
"Why, God? Why?"
Oh, how I loved him
Adored him
My arms ache
In loving
For just a moment
To hold him
Close to my heart
In this so-called
Physical material world
He was real
Oh so real
Deep swelling pain
Overwhelms me
My senses alive...
Yet dead
I ask "why" again...
Again and again
But no answer comes
In grief
I collapse
Hopeless...helpless
A fool

Lost...he's lost
Is this the end?
Nothing more?
But no...
A glimmer has appeared
Before my eyes
A voice so tender
Gentle and inviting
"You will hold him
In eternity
As a mother should"

STRUGGLE

Alone, so alone
Darkness overwhelms
Silence reigns supreme
Clouds blaspheme
The sky above
Traps, pits
Falling, falling
All around
Slipping into nothingness
Fire consumes
My soul
Retching, burning
Walking coals
Rolling about
Path so straight
Yet crooked
Mortified
My soul burns
Envious for peace
Alluring
Out of reach
Yet in sight
Teasing, tempting
Light withdraws
Not deserved
Punishment reigns
Supreme
He laughs
A raucous sound
Haunting
Darkest of souls
No hope

No glory
No relief
Light beckons
Arms outstretched
A hand
I see a hand
Reaching down
Lighting the clouds
Climbing the ladder
I am grabbed
Pulled to safety
Forever, evermore

STRUGGLE 2

Cracking, thin walls
Banging, banging
Laughter emanating through
Banging harder
But it will not break
Alone – so alone
Depression pours down
Drenching me
Hair mattes my face
Banging, banging
Walls crack
Thickening to my touch
Laughter evades me
Pushing, pressing
All there is is pain
Aching, laughable
Nobody cares
They keep laughing
Beyond the walls
Trapping me

HOPELESSNESS

Walls, walls, walls!
Everywhere walls!
Punching the paper-mache
The first is broken
I stride forward
Brown-red bricks face me
Punching one I bleed
Throwing myself I break my body
Screeching in pain
Battling the struggle
I push on
Bricks move slowly
Then fall about me
Deafening noise assails me
Stumbling through the bloody mess
I approach the final wall
Cement
Slouching to the ground
Overly weakened
I give up

WHO I AM

Into the misty moors
Beckoning, calling
I hear my name
A whisper in the fog
Consoling, soothing
Comforting
Black birds twirl
Crows, vultures
Encircle me, waiting
A howl cries out
In the midst
Skies above
Unseen by fog
All is black, grey
No light
Brightening my path
Deep pits, thorny bushes
Pain, blood
This is my life
Take it, leave it
It's who I am
Leave me be.

MY PAIN

Pain
Uplifting, arousing
Pleasure
Coils my soil
Muting
Within heart strings
Right, wrong
Who's to judge?
I choose
For me
No one else
My life, my body
My pain
Agony
Overwhelming
Spinning, twisting
What is truth?
Somewhere deep
My own truth
Don't deny me
Heart, mind, soul
They speak
What is true
My truth
Is real
Very

SELF PORTRAIT

What do you see
Gazing in my eyes?
Laughter, joy
Spirit, tears?
Perhaps a woman
A kind hearted soul
Confused, lost
She hides it well
Emotional, real
Honest, true
It is all a veil
Rainbow gauze
Alternating grey, black
Within
Do you truly see her?
The pain, the terror
The madness?
Crying in secret
Tearing out her hair
No one knows her
Not really
She hides it well
The killer within.

IN MY HEAD

Yelping, howling
Cry all you want
No one hears
No one listens
All alone
Alone
My pain, all mine
None to share
None to comprehend
Crazy
Yes you are
Psychotic, insane
World is spinning
Unreal
What is reality?
The truth
In my head
My own world
Personal realm
Mystical, fantastic
Nightmarish
Rainbow hues
Black, grey, white
Fantasy
My only friend

PASSION

O breath of life
Seduce me
Milky white
Pure, smooth
Caress me
My love
Desire overwhelms
Beating hearts
As one
Your touch
So gentle
Titillating
Full pleasure
Awaits
Tracing fingers
Delicately
Barely touching
Tender kisses
Most private places
Lust, desire
Take me
I am yours
Slave

YOUR LOVE

Consume me
Beseech me
Throw me
Into the
Fiery furnace
Of your
Undying love
You, you alone
No other
I want
Only you
My desire, my heart
Is yours, yours alone
Take me- now
Fill my heart
With your soul
Your desire
Gaze back
Back at me
You are in me
I am in you
Grab me up
While I yet
Live, love
For you
And you alone

LOVE ALONE

Love
So mysterious
Evasive
Where is it?
I keep
Missing the X
Faded marks
Nowhere seen
I admire
Lovers
All around
Yet I, I am
Alone
In this world
Missing the X
Tears me apart
Pulling my hair
Strands fall
Clumps
In my hands
So ugly
So unlovable
Alone
Ever after

CHANGE

Butterfly wings
Stretching, birthing
Breaking through
Cocoon webs
Hanging on
Tree of life
Existence
It flourishes
Fluttering once, twice
Taking off
Amongst
Wildflowers, daffodils
Waving in the breezes
Of utopia
Wings so light
Translucent
Sapphire, ruby
Gold
Emerald eyes
Dart about
Flexing, reaching
Flying high, higher
Life is grand
Such beauty
All it knows
For all time

NECTAR OF LIFE

Tree sap
Ruby red
Dripping, dripping
Mother's blood
For the tiny child
Standing on toes
Hugging the tree
She tilts her head
Mouth open wide
Sap hits
Her tongue
Tinging her
Precious little lips
Now red as
Blood lipstick
Black eyes shine
Brushing raven hair
Away
From the sap
Mother coos
Whispering
Drink your fill
My little one
Today's treat is
Precious as life.

TRAPPED IN MEMORIES

Agony
Chills my heart
My soul shivers
Pain so intense
Melts the ice
Trying to form
To protect
Breaking, breaking down
I cling to
Memories
Yet
Wanting, wishing to
Forget them
Feelings so strong
Overpowering
Overwhelming
I lose control
Lose myself
Screaming, screeching
No!!
Help me!!
I can't take this
Anymore
Whimpering
Begging
Free me
Please

LOST LOVE

Come to me
All who mourn
Grieving life
Unfulfilled
Full of pain
Regret, guilt
Shame
For you are
Loved, yes loved
Truth shall
Reign
Lies, falsehoods
Disappear
Fade away
In my embrace
My children
My beloved ones
Never, never
Will I
Let you go
We are one
You and I
Spirit bound
Live, live I say
You are healed
By my breath
Spread your wing
And fly
Fly my beloved

DEATH'S CALL

Time reveals
Exposes
All secrets
No matter
How dark
What will
They say, do
Abandon me
Run far away
I am
Rotten fruit
Damaged
Crazy, psycho
Keep away
I am
A bad person
Evil
To the core
Death beckons
I'll be free
When gone
Dead
Forever
No more
Torture
I am
Death itself

SURVIVING

Wind swept
I trudge on
Through torment
Sands of time
Burn blades
Across my face
Sun scorched
Burning red
Bleeding ruby
I trudge on
Beneath
Freezing stars
Ice pebbles
Slip beneath me
Head hooded
Face veiled
I trudge on
Still
Glass swords
Strike
My hands, my legs
Determined
I trudge on
Bleeding, aching
Forcing myself
Continue on
Within sight
My goal
I trudge on

COMPASSION

Please my love
Do not despair
I love, adore you
My life, my mate
Turn your frown
Upside down
Bunny, bunny
Hop, hop, hop
From my mind
To yours
We belong
Together
Forever
I am here
For you
My love
Open up
Share your pain
With me
Let me
Embrace you
With my heart
Wipe your tears
Your sadness
Is mine
Please smile
My love
You are
Never alone.

FOREVERMORE

Love beckons
A quandary
Is it real,
True?
Is death
The end all?
Will love
Cease to exist?
Or is it
Eternal
Beyond infinity
Soulful, begging
Searching always
For the one
Or the many
Who will
Fulfill her
Destiny
Infinite cycles
Of life
Breeding love
Between
Joined souls
There is
No end
Only
Forevermore

DISCOVERY

Who am I?
Where am I?
What am I?
No-
Not right
How am I?
There, there
The answers
Lie in wait
Happy, sad
Grouchy, cheery
No-
Those
Do not
Define
Look within
Better yet-
Feel, feel
What's within
Your heart, soul
Is your spirit
Soaring or diving?
Flip and wave
Dive deep
Deep within
You will
Find your
True self
Waiting.

JOURNEY

Life
Leads us
Down many
Paths
Light, dark
Joyful, sad
Bridges are
Crossed
Pebbles kicked
Rocks lifted
Footprints
On this earth
In hearts
Yes, in hearts
Where we
Abide
In loved ones'
Lives
We are
Never alone
Someone cares
Someone
Out there
Whether
In sight
Or not
They hold
Alight
When ours is
Out
Forever.

BLINDLY SEEKING

Crawling about
Unseen, hidden
In shadows
Many, many eyes
Staring
My way
Searching
Wondering
Where is she?
Where did she go?
But do they
Really care?
I think not
They only look
With their
Eyes
Not their
Hearts, souls
Looking right
At me, through me
Their search is
Hopeless
Hearts in the
Wrong place
Seek me out
Truly
Seek the
Real me
I am
Waiting
Right here
If you
Care

TAKE ME AS I AM

So what
If I'm
Different

This is me
I am not
You

Let me
Be me

I will not
Be controlled

I will not
Be told
What to
Believe

Do not
Tell me
Who I am
Is wrong

Accept me

I will
Not change

Embracing
Myself

I am finally
Set free

Joy fills
My heart

Laughter is
My song

Take me
As I am

Or leave me
Be

SHATTERED PLANS

Trapped
Isolated
You think
I chose this?
No!
Crippled
Exhausted
Day to day
Unknown
Make plans
Excited
Getting out
BAM!!
Pain
Exhaustion
Weakness
Overbearing
Plans are
Cancelled
Last minute
Trapped
Caged
Lonely
Alone
Misunderstood
I cry
And cry

ISOLATED TEARS

I hate this
Trapped
In body
Trapped
In mind
Daily struggles
Forced
Isolation
No one
Understands
No one
Can relate
They think
I choose
This life
I want to
Scream
But who would
Hear me?
Who would
Actually listen
So I
Curl up
Within
Myself
Weeping
Crying
I am
Alone
In my
Pain and
Suffering

PRECIOUS CHILD

Emily my dear
My sweet precious
Angel of mine
Come to me, come to me
I miss you so
Fragrant wildflowers
Fill the air about me
I know you are here
O my precious little
Angel of mine
My love for you is
Infinite, beyond eternity
Let me feel your touch
Place your fragile hand
On mine
Our hearts beat in rhythm
As one soul, one being
I want to hold you
In my arms forever
And ever
I need you my precious
One day we will join
Forevermore
I know this
In my heart.

BLESSINGS

Life is a blessing
Truly it is
True, there are
Hardships to endure
Sorrow and pain
Yet joy can overcome
It comes from within
Look deep inside
You are alive
There is so, so much
To be grateful for
Think on it
Even minor, silly things
Such as toilet paper
Imagine life without it
People do care about you
Though you may not have
Experienced love
It is there, everywhere
Yes, rock bottom agonizes
Deep into your soul
Yet hope persists
Life is the answer
Life deep within for
Life is a blessing

EVERYWHERE

Monsters within
Monsters without
Looking there then there
Everywhere, they are everywhere
No hiding, no hiding
Within or without
Curling up in a ball
Covering my head
I cry till I drown
No escape
No, never can escape
They are my constant companions
Monsters within
Monsters without
Living in constant fear
Because of them
I can never escape
Their endless presence
Monsters within
Monsters without

THE DANCER

Oh how morose!
Can you believe it?
Again, and yet again

She spins and swirls
Rainbows of colors
Twirling in ribbons
About her little body

Neverending, ever
On and on she goes
Muscles taut but free
Dainty feet barely touching
As they fly about the floor

Dancing and leaping
Twisting in every which way

The music plays on
Her dainty feet bleeding
Upon the broken glass floor

Yet she goes on
And on.

LIFE CYCLES

Time rolls on
An infinite web
Of deceit and fate

There is no end
Battles rage on
Evil wins, good wins

Nothing pure exists
Lies come and go
Truths fade

We live on
Life after life
Torture and blessings

Energy cycles
One way, then another
Always swirling

Never ending
Never changing
Forever and ever